Red Hot in Amsterdam

A play

Patricia Robinson

Samuel French—London
New York-Toronto-Hollywood

Copyright ©1999 by Samuel French
All Rights Reserved

RED HOT IN AMSTERDAM is fully protected under the copyright laws of the British Commonwealth, including Canada, the United States of America, and all other countries of the Copyright Union. All rights, including professional and amateur stage productions, recitation, lecturing, public reading, motion picture, radio broadcasting, television and the rights of translation into foreign languages are strictly reserved.

ISBN 978-0-573-12218-7

www.samuelfrench-london.co.uk

www.samuelfrench.com

FOR AMATEUR PRODUCTION ENQUIRIES

UNITED KINGDOM AND WORLD EXCLUDING NORTH AMERICA

plays@SamuelFrench-London.co.uk

020 7255 4302/01

Each title is subject to availability from Samuel French, depending upon country of performance.

CAUTION: Professional and amateur producers are hereby warned that RED HOT IN AMSTERDAM is subject to a licensing fee. Publication of this play does not imply availability for performance. Both amateurs and professionals considering a production are strongly advised to apply to the appropriate agent before starting rehearsals, advertising, or booking a theatre. A licensing fee must be paid whether the title is presented for charity or gain and whether or not admission is charged.

The professional rights in this play are controlled by Samuel French Ltd, 52 Fitzroy Street, London, W1T 5JR

No one shall make any changes in this title for the purpose of production. No part of this book may be reproduced, stored in a retrieval system, or transmitted in any form, by any means, now known or yet to be invented, including mechanical, electronic, photocopying, recording, videotaping, or otherwise, without the prior written permission of the publisher. No one shall upload this title, or part of this title, to any social media websites.

The right of Patricia Robinson to be identified as author of this work has been asserted in accordance with Section 77 of the Copyright, Designs and Patents Act 1988.

RED HOT IN AMSTERDAM

First performed at The Arts Centre, St Helier, Jersey, in September 1998, with the following cast:

Corrine	Pat Bisson
Kora	Olivia de Gruchy
Frank	Mark Poisson
Mickey	David Mahe
Madame Celestine	Caroline Le Maistre
Chief Inspector	Tim Allen
Thief	Phillipa Burnett

The play was directed by **Pat Bisson**
Lighting and set design by **Mike Wynes**
Set dressing and design by **Simon Thomas** and **Denise Renouf**

COPYRIGHT INFORMATION
(See also page ii)

This play is fully protected under the Copyright Laws of the British Commonwealth of Nations, the United States of America and all countries of the Berne and Universal Copyright Conventions.

All rights, including Stage, Motion Picture, Radio, Television, Public Reading, and Translation into Foreign Languages, are strictly reserved.

No part of this publication may lawfully be reproduced in ANY form or by any means — photocopying, typescript, recording (including video-recording), manuscript, electronic, mechanical, or otherwise — or be transmitted or stored in a retrieval system, without prior permission.

Licences are issued subject to the understanding that it shall be made clear in all advertising matter that the audience will witness an amateur performance; that the names of the authors of the plays shall be included on all announcements and on all programmes; and that the integrity of the authors' work will be preserved.

The Royalty Fee is subject to contract and subject to variation at the sole discretion of Samuel French Ltd.

In Theatres or Halls seating Four Hundred or more the fee will be subject to negotiation.

In Territories Overseas the fee quoted in this Acting Edition may not apply. A fee will be quoted on application to our local authorized agent, or if there is no such agent, on application to Samuel French Ltd, London.

VIDEO-RECORDING OF AMATEUR PRODUCTIONS

Please note that the copyright laws governing video-recording are extremely complex and that it should not be assumed that any play may be video-recorded for *whatever purpose* without first obtaining the permission of the appropriate agents. The fact that a play is published by Samuel French Ltd does not indicate that video rights are available or that Samuel French Ltd controls such rights.

CHARACTERS

Corrine, a French prostitute
Kora, a Dutch prostitute
Frank, a British burglar
Mickey, a British burglar
Madame Celestine
Chief of Police
Man (Thief)

The action of the play takes place in the parlour of Madame Celestine's Sex Shop in the Red Light District of Amsterdam

Time: the present

An optional prologue takes place in the prostitutes'"windows"

Prologue

Optional comic mime scene

If this scene is included the setting needs to be expanded to show the two prostitutes' "windows" - perhaps one each side of the main setting, taking the form of large (empty) picture frames with the girls one side and the street on the other (auditorium side)

Music plays as the Curtain opens. The Lights come up on Corrine, a French "woman of the night"

Corrine is seated in her window R and is making up her face in a compact mirror. As she does so she notices a potential client at the window. She blows him a kiss, stands and puts her foot on the chair and adjusts her stockings to tease him. She then parades a little and gestures at how much she costs. He refuses. She is angry. She then has an idea. She turns her back to the street, wiggles her bottom, turns again, and to her delight counts five men at her window

The Lights go down on Corrine and come up on Kora, a Dutch "woman of the night"

Kora is seated and looking rather fed up. She spots a potential client at her window and parades herself. She takes off her leather belt, puts her foot up on the chair and slaps her leg lightly with the belt. She gestures at her cost. The client refuses, she argues with him, and makes a rude gesture

The Lights fade

RED HOT IN AMSTERDAM

Scene 1

The parlour of Madame Celestine's Sex Shop in the Red Light District, Amsterdam. Night

There is a settee, a table with an empty vase on it, a chair, a waste basket, a drinks bar, and a mantelpiece. On the mantelpiece is an urn and a pot containing an artificial plant. There is an open window to the rear or side of the stage and a front door

A police chase is heard off stage: sirens blaring, car doors slamming and footsteps running, getting closer and closer, and finally coming to a halt in the alleyway of the back entrance to the shop

Frank and Mickey, both British, are puffing and panting as they speak

Frank (*off*) They've got us surrounded, we'll never make it! What are we going to do?
Mickey (*off*) There's only one thing to do—look! Up there! An open window! Let's get in, quick!

Dustbins rattle as they clamber on to them

Frank's face appears at the window first, while Mickey, the smaller of the two, has difficulty maintaining the height and keeps disappearing

Is it all clear?

Frank Yeah. There's nobody about.
Mickey (*off*) Good, now hoist me on your shoulders.

Frank's face drops out of sight. Puffing and panting, and with a rattle of dustbins, each hushing up the other, Mickey's face appears. He sways from side to side

Keep still, you great bullock. I can't get a grip!
Frank (*off*) You've got your boot in my face!
Mickey I'll put my boot somewhere else if you don't get me in here right now! Now push! (*With immense effort and determination, he scrambles in through the window and falls on to the floor*) Come on!

Frank clambers in with the help of Mickey

They scurry across the floor and hide in front of the settee. Footsteps are heard running off stage, lights flash, then the footsteps become fainter

Frank I think they're going.
Mickey Ssh!

The footsteps disappear into the distance

Frank They've gone! We're safe!

They pause to catch their breath

Cor, this place pongs like a sumo wrestler's jock strap! Where do you think we are?
Mickey How the hell should I know! You're the navigator—so navigate.

Frank looks at him blankly

Look at the map.

Scene 1

Frank Oh yeah. (*He takes a map from his pocket*) Er... Now I think we're ... er ... er...

Mickey (*snatching it from him*) Give me that. Look! There's Central Station and the dam—right? That building there—that's the factory where we nicked the diamonds—right? We took a right and a left—then another left—straight across the junction, along the canal, passed the Floating Flower Market, that's when we started to leg it. We took another right—a left—another right, then went down 'ere into the alley, which means we're right—'ere—right?

Frank (*confused*) Right—where?

Mickey There, stupid! The—Ach-ter-burg-wal.

Frank The Achter what?

Mickey The Red Light District.

Frank Red Light District! You mean—this place is a brothel?

Mickey You got it in one, my son.

Frank Cor! That's a bit o' luck!

Mickey Forget the tarts, Frank, we've got more important things to think about, like how we're going to get back to the UK with two million quid's worth of uncut diamonds and the whole of the bleeding Amsterdam police force looking for us.

Frank Yeah. What are we going to do?

Mickey I don't know! (*He pauses*) Wait! I've got an idea!

Frank Yeah?

Mickey We'll dump the diamonds.

Frank Dump 'em! But Mickey, we've only just nicked 'em!

Mickey Not dump them for good, stupid! Dump them for the time being. Look, the streets are swarming with police; they'll pick us up in no time, but if we cause a bit of bother, get picked up and searched and don't have the ice on us, they'll have to let us go. Then we'll come back, pick up the diamonds, and be back in London before they've had time to stamp our passports.

Frank They don't stamp passports any more, Mickey.

Mickey I know that, stupid—I was talking metaphorically-like, right?

Frank (*unsure*) Oh right! What if one of the tarts finds 'em?

Mickey They won't if we hide them in the right place. Now let's think of somewhere nobody will look.

Voices are heard off stage

Frank Someone's coming!
Mickey Christ! Stick 'em in the bottom of that plant pot quick—and make sure they're well hidden.

Frank stuffs the diamond pouch in the artificial plant pot

Quick! Let's get out of here!

They both try to get out of the window at the same time, unsuccessfully

Careful, you great pillock! Look, you go first, then you can catch me if I fall.
Frank Right, Mickey.

Frank and Mickey exit clumsily

Noises of a dustbin crashing, a cat's hiss and meow, and moaning and groaning as they fall

Corrine enters. She checks no-one is looking then crosses to the bar to get a drink. As she is pouring it Kora enters and makes her jump

Kora hears the commotion outside and crosses to the window to look out. Corrine reclines in a chair

Kora There is so much noise tonight. Police sirens, light flashing... (*She sees Mickey and Frank*) There are some men below the window!
Corrine Ignore it, chérie! It will be the usual perverts and drug addicts.
Kora (*shouting through the window*) Clear off, you scumbags. Do your snorting elsewhere!

Footsteps are heard running into the distance. Kora, tough and used to such things, dismisses the incident immediately. She walks down stage, rubbing her back, and sits down

I refuse to sit any more in that window. My legs they ache, my body it aches, my head it aches...
Corrine Oh, stop complaining, it is all you ever do. If you had as many customers as me to satisfy—then you would ache.
Kora Are you saying that you have more customers than me?
Corrine Of course. I am much prettier than you, that is why I have more customers.
Kora Prettier! Your face has more lines on it than the French Metro.
Corrine Huh! You Dutch are so dumb-dumb, you could not even find your way to the Central Station in Amsterdam.
Kora At least I am not over-screwed and over the hill like you.
Corrine (*standing*) Oh! You are diabolique! I am tired of working with you Dutch whores. You are so cold and insensitive.
Kora And you French are so naïve and stupid.
Corrine Oh! You—you are nothing but—Euro Trash! (*She picks up the plant pot containing the diamonds and hurls it towards Kora*)

As it hits the floor, the diamond pouch falls out and the girls make a dive for it

Kora It's mine! Give it to me!
Corrine I found it first! Take your filthy trashy hands off it!
Kora I said it's mine!
Corrine There! I have it! (*She looks inside and gasps*)
Kora What is it, Corrine? What do you see?

Corrine is speechless

Oh, give it to me. (*She snatches the pouch and looks inside*) Diamonds! There must be millions of guilder worth of diamonds here. Where did they come from?
Corrine I do not know. Do you think they belong to Madame Celestine?

Kora Idiot! Why would Madame Celestine hide diamonds in a plant pot? If she wanted to hide them she would put them in a safer place than that.
Corrine Then to who do they belong? Who put them there—and why?
Kora You think I am the mind reader? (*Inspired*) Perhaps somebody stole them and hid them in here.
Corrine But who?
Kora I do not know that! How would I know that? (*She pauses*) The men in the alley!
Corrine You think *they* hid the diamonds?
Kora It is possible. The police were chasing somebody, we heard the sirens. Perhaps they came in through the window to hide, then heard us coming, panicked, hid the diamonds and made their escape.
Corrine It is possible... It is possible. What shall we do? Shall we tell Madame Celestine?
Kora Why should we do that? Would she tell us if she had found diamonds? No, she would not and we will not tell her. I shall keep them in my valise until I decide what to do with them.
Corrine You will not! I found them, they are my diamonds, I will keep them in my valise until I decide what to do with them. (*She snatches them from Kora*)

Kora snatches them back

Kora You French whore, I saw them fall on the floor first—the diamonds belong to me!
Corrine And if I had not thrown the plant pot at you, you would never have seen them fall on the floor—they are my diamonds!
Kora No! They are mine! Get your hands off them!

A tug of war begins

Oh! This is so stupid! We will split the diamonds.
Corrine Split them?

Scene 1

Kora Half for you and half for me? At fifty per cent we will still be rich beyond our dreams.
Corrine (*unconvinced*) Very well, but *I* will count the diamonds and distribute them to you.
Kora No. We will count and distribute them together, but not now, Madame will be looking for us soon.
Corrine When?
Kora On Sunday, when Madame goes to her church. I will look after them until then.
Corrine (*snatching them from her*) You will not! I will look after them.
Kora (*snatching them back*) French bitch!
Corrine (*snatching them back*) Dutch cow!

They begin to fight

Madame Celestine enters

Madame Girls! Girls! What is going on here?

The girls jump apart abruptly. Corrine hides the diamond pouch behind her back

Kora Madam Celestine! I... She...
Corrine She... I... We...
Madame Why are you gabbling so and why are you not sitting in the window, drumming up the trade, as you should be?
Corrine It was she, Madame... Kora... She said that she ached very badly. I came to help her. I was about to get her a little brandy... I...
Madame Is that so, Kora? Are you not well?
Kora I... I ... do have a headache, Madame, and a touch of the stomach ache.
Madame Tsk! Tsk! That is not good.
Kora It is nothing, Madame, it will be gone by the morning.
Madame I hope so. In the meantime, you must have your glass of

brandy, it is very good for the settling of the stomach. (*She crosses to the bar*)

Corrine quickly drops the diamond pouch into the vase on the table

What do you think has brought on these sudden aches and pains, Kora?

Kora I—I ... am not sure, Madame. Perhaps it was my client last night, he insisted on having the window open. The bed is near the window and the night air was chilly, so it is possible...

Madame It is not necessary to say more. I understand. (*She hands Kora her drink*)

Kora Thank you, Madame.

Madame (*sighing*) I must confess I didn't expect it to happen quite so soon to you, Kora, I would have hoped for a few more years.

Kora Madame?

Madame Age has obviously come upon you quite suddenly.

Kora Age!

Madame Do not be alarmed, Kora, we are all aware that women have a shelf life. Unfortunately, your shelf has gathered dust quicker than others. I am afraid I have no choice but to discontinue your employment.

Kora But, Madame, I am not too old!

Madame Aching bones, headaches, tiredness, it is a sure sign that you're getting too old and there is no room in my shop for has-beens. Is that not right, Corrine?

Corrine Absolutely, Madame. She is too old.

Kora You French bitch, you are older than I am!

Corrine Liar!

Kora You are thirty if you are a day.

Corrine At least I am not shrivelled where it matters. You are a Dutch prune.

Madame Girls! Girls! Enough! Enough! I will not allow fighting in my establishment! Get back to your posts at once. I do not want to hear another word about sickness. If you vomit—you

Scene 1

vomit. If your head hurts—it hurts. If your neck is stiff—close the window. If nothing else is stiff—work harder. Now go.

Kora \
Corrine } (*together*) Yes, Madame.

Kora and Corrine exit

Madame crosses to the mantelpiece and lovingly touches the urn. She begins to talk to it

Madame Did you hear that, George my darling? Lazy creatures! They bring me in so little money—they are worthless. (*She pauses*) Oh George! There is so much pornography around these days it is ruining my business. I cannot make ends meet... If only I could get my hands on a large amount of money. Do you think you can help me, my darling? Could you, by some miracle, enable me to get more money?

The doorbell rings

(*Kissing the urn*) Do try my darling. (*She opens the door*)

The Chief of Police enters. He is looking very sour and unhappy. Behind his back he is holding a bunch of flowers

Chief Inspector!
Chief Madame Celestine.
Madame Come in! Come in! What a nice surprise, I was not expecting to see you this evening.
Chief I was not expecting to be here, Madame, but something terrible happened and ... and... (*He is overcome and cannot go on*)
Madame Chief Inspector, are you not well?
Chief I am well. (*He gives her the flowers*) For you, Madame.
Madame Flowers! Why, Chief Inspector, never before have you brought me flowers! For what is the occasion?
Chief No occasion, Madame. I cannot tell the lie. The flowers

were for my wife. I have been spending too much time away from her and have not been in her good books of late, so I decided to surprise her. I left the station early to buy the flowers. My intention was to enjoy with her a romantic candlelight dinner at the Frascati, but when I got to my home... (*He is too overcome to carry on*)

Madame Sit down, Inspector... Sit down...

Chief I am sorry. It has been rather traumatic for me.

Madame Your wife. She is well?

Chief She looked very well when I left, very well indeed. She was in the arms of another man.

Madame No!

Chief Yes!

Madame What deceit!

Chief Terrible. It is the truth to say that I, Chief Inspector Andre of the Amsterdam Police Department, and father of four children, was astounded and humiliated by her infidelity.

Madame I too am astounded. But I am pleased that you came here, to my establishment, to seek solace and comfort.

Chief It is indeed solace and comfort that I need, Madame.

Madame And solace and comfort you will receive. I have never let you down before and I will not begin now. (*She flicks through her book*) Now let me see ... what about Angelique?

Chief (*smiling*) The leather and the whip?

Madame Yes.

Chief (*frowning*) Too strenuous. I am feeling traumatised after seeing my wife... I don't think the whip...

Madame Of course! I am not thinking clearly. I too am traumatised by your wife's deceit... Ah! Jacqueline?

Chief (*smiling*) The plastic and the umbrella?

Madame And the rubber wellingtons.

Chief (*frowning*) Too cold! I feel the need for warmth and comfort. Seeing my wife with another man ... it has—chilled me to the bone.

Madame Oh, but I am such a fool and so insensitive. Ah! I have just the person you are looking for! There can be nobody better for you in your traumatic state than Marie Claire.

Scene 1

Chief (*smiling*) The feathers...?
Madame And the honey.
Chief Wonderful!
Madame Good. I am so thrilled to be able to help you in your hour of such need. She is in number six window at present, go straight in.
Chief Thank you, Madame. You are most kind. I am sure it will take my mind off the scenario in my home.
Madame Marie Claire is trained to do that very thing, Inspector. You will soon forget everything.

The Chief exits

Madame crosses to the bar and pours a little water into a jug which she takes to the vase containing the diamonds. As she does so, she talks to her dead husband

It is terrible, is it not, my darling? What kind of a wife would cheat on her husband? Tsk! What is the world coming too? I do hope Marie Claire is up to her usual standard and can take his mind off his wife's indiscretion. (*She realizes that something is in the vase and puts her hand inside. She brings out the pouch and looks inside. When she sees the diamonds she believes that her dead husband has answered her call for help*) Diamonds! But how? Who? (*She looks at the urn*) Oh George! George, my darling! How did you manage to do this so quickly? I am overwhelmed with gratitude. I would have preferred guilders but I am not complaining. I will soon sell them, but to whom? I will make certain enquiries. But for the moment I must hide them. Where shall I hide them, my darling? Where? Ah! Of course! Where better than in your safe keeping. You, my sweet darling, can look after them for me. (*She puts the diamonds into the urn, kisses it and puts it back*) Take care of them for me, my darling.

Black-out

Scene 2

Early the following evening. Dim lighting

The flowers are now in the vase on the table

Noises off stage. Footsteps. Dustbins clang, lots of whispering

Frank and Mickey appear at the window and clamber inside

Mickey You stay here and keep a look-out. I'll get the diamonds. (*He crosses to the plant pot and puts his hand inside*) What the...
Frank What's up?
Mickey They've gone! The diamonds have gone!
Frank (*clambering in*) Are you sure?
Mickey 'Course I'm sure. Some bastard's nicked 'em!
Frank I don't like it, Mickey. Let's forget the diamonds and get out of here while we still can.
Mickey Forget the diamonds! Are you kidding? Look, sunshine, I'm not letting some tart with silicon mammaries steal two million quid's worth of diamonds from under my nose. If you want to go—go. I'm staying.

Frank crosses to the window, but changes his mind

Frank I'm not leaving you, Mickey, we're in this together. What are we going to do?
Mickey I don't know yet. I've got to think... I've got to think! I've got it! Follow me!

Mickey isn't quite sure which way to exit; he turns L and then exits R, followed by Frank

Madame enters, humming with happiness

She checks inside the urn, kisses it, and is about to pour herself a drink when the doorbell rings. She opens the door

Scene 2

The Chief of Police enters

Chief Good evening, Madame Celestine.
Madame Chief Inspector! Come in! Come in! Two evenings in a row. I am honoured. Who would you like this evening ... Jacquie—Anoushka...?
Chief Unfortunately my visit this evening is not of a personal nature, it is on official business that I call.
Madame Official business! But I have done nothing wrong, I have paid all bills, I have paid all protection monies... Is it my girls? Have they been behaving badly again? If so, I shall speak to them immediately...
Chief It is not your girls, Madame. My visit concerns a robbery.
Madame A robbery?
Chief That is what I said, yes.
Madame What kind of a robbery, Chief Inspector?
Chief It involves a large amount of precious stones.
Madame Precious stones?
Chief That is what I said, yes. To be exact—diamonds.
Madame Diamonds! (*She is so shocked she almost faints*)
Chief Madame, you look quite faint, perhaps you should sit down.
Madame Yes... Yes, I think you are right. Thank you.

He helps her on to the settee

But why have you come to my humble establishment, Chief Inspector? Surely you do not think that somebody here is responsible for the theft?
Chief Of course not. Do not worry yourself about that, but two suspects were pursued by my men into this area. They ran into the alleyway, which the back of your shop faces and they have not been seen since.
Madame Y-you think they could be—here?
Chief Two thoughts cross my mind, Madame; one—the thieves could have disposed of the diamonds with thought of regaining them later to make their getaway; two—they could be in hiding with the diamonds. I must try to cover all possibilities, you understand.

Madame Yes, yes, of course. You are most thorough, that is why you are the Chief of Police, is it not?

Chief Exactly, Madame. Now, if my first scenario is correct, then the question on my lips is, where would the villains have hidden the diamonds?

Madame I am at a loss to help you with your answer.

Chief My expectations of you are not so high as all that. Madame, after all, I am the Chief of Police and you are a mere brothel keeper, are you not?

Madame (*hurt*) I suppose you could say that, yes.

Chief And if they did hide the diamonds, my next question is—when will they come back for them?

Madame Come back!

Chief It follows, does it not? They would not leave Amsterdam without the diamonds. That is why it is important that we discover the whereabouts of the diamonds and are lying in wait when they return to collect them.

Madame I—I see.

Chief Unfortunately, Madame Celestine, we must search all the premises in this area. My men are searching as I speak. It will take them a long time, of course.

Madame nods knowingly

But as you are a personal friend of mine, I shall search your premises myself. You have no objection to that?

Madame Of course not, Chief Inspector. I am only delighted that it is you who will conduct the search.

Chief Where, then, would you like me to begin?

Madame If—if you would like to begin in Angelique's room—number nine, I will be with you shortly.

Chief Ah, Angelique—a very good place to begin a thorough search, Madame.

TheChief exits L

Madame rushes to the urn and speaks to it

Scene 2

Madame George! George! I know you were only trying to help me, but did they have to be stolen diamonds? What am I to do? What am I to do? (*She listens intently*) Pardon, my darling? No—no, of course not, I shall not give them in to the Chief Inspector and I will stay calm, I promise. (*She breathes deeply*) See—I am now calm. Oh, I do not know what to do... I must think... I must think...

Madame exits with the urn

Frank and Mickey enter. Frank is dressed as an erotic female Viking Queen, complete with whip. Mickey is draped from head to foot in flowing white with only his eyes showing. Frank is not at all happy

Frank There's no way this scam is going to work! No way!
Mickey 'Course it'll work. We look tastier than the tarts in the window.
Frank Are you a bit Brahms and Liszt or something?
Mickey Trust me, Frank, we look great. Nobody would know we were blokes.
Frank I've gotta have a drink. (*He crosses to the bar with a manly walk*)
Mickey For Christ's sake, Frank, you're supposed to be a tart!
Frank What do you mean?
Mickey You've got to walk like a tart, not a bloke.
Frank But I am a bloke and I can't walk like a tart.
Mickey 'Course you can. If tarts can do it, it's got to be easy. Look, all you have to do is walk like this. (*He puts his hand on his hips and swaggers and sways around the stage like a woman*) Easy. Now you try it.
Frank Get off! I'm not walking like that!
Mickey Yes, you are!
Frank No, I'm not!
Mickey Let me put it to you this way, my old son. Do you want to be rich and spend the rest of your life lying on a beach in the Caribbean surrounded by sun-tanned, leggy tarts or do you want

to spend the next twenty years in a cold bleak cell in Amsterdam with not a skirt in sight?

Frank pauses to think, then puts his hands on his hips and begins walking like a female

Frank How's this?
Mickey Yeah! That's it. You've got it!
Frank (*stopping*) And I ain't giving any of it away neither.
Mickey I ain't asking you to. Oh, there is one other thing—your voice.
Frank What's wrong with my voice?
Mickey It's a bit deep for a tart.
Frank Deep?
Mickey Yeah. It needs to be higher—like this... (*High pitched*) Hallo! I'm Veronica, the Virgin Queen... What can I do for you?
Frank That's it! I'm off! (*He heads for the window*)

Mickey stops him

Mickey Frankie, my son. Think of the Caribbean.
Frank We'll never get away with it.
Mickey "Course we will! Now you have a quick shuftie round here while I case a couple of the rooms.
Frank No! Mickey! Come back! Don't leave me ... not like this...

Mickey exits

Frank is terrified and doesn't know what to do with himself. He starts to practise his female walk

The Chief Inspector enters. He watches Frank with lustful interest

Frank attempts a little pirouette, after which the Chief applauds

Scene 2

Chief Bravo!

Frank is stiff with fright and only his eyeballs move. The Chief moves closer to him

Do not be afraid, my little one, I am only admiring you. Are you new?

Frank makes a pitiful whining sound

Ah! I see, you are new to Madame's shop. (*He whispers in his ear*) I don't suppose you are a virgin?

Frank whines louder

I didn't think you were, I was merely hoping. What is your name? Speak up, my dear. Have you nothing to say?
Frank (*high pitched voice*) Hallo! My name is Veronica—the Viking Queen.
Chief (*lustily*) The Viking Queen! I can see why!
Frank (*gruffly*) What can I...? (*He clears his throat and talks in a high tone*) What can I do for you?

The Chief saunters around Frank and touches him as he speaks. Frank's whine becomes louder still

Chief I am sure you can do a lot for me. Those shoulders, those arms, those thighs... such muscles. You must have been body-building to achieve such a shape as this.
Frank Not body-building... Boxing.
Chief Boxing!
Frank Yes. (*He flirts outrageously*) Would you like to see my right hook?
Chief I would love to see your right hook.

Frank lands a right hook and the Chief hits the deck. Frank drags him out of sight

Frank exits with his skirt between his legs

Mickey enters

Mickey I've searched the bottom floor, I can't find anything... Frank... Frank... Where the hell are you...? Frank...

Madame enters, with the urn, looking very concerned. She doesn't see Mickey. She kisses the urn and replaces it on the mantelpiece

Mickey, on seeing Madame, tries to tiptoe past her to exit

Madame George... George... This is setting my teeth on the edge but I am staying calm as you suggest... But my darling, it is such a strain, I need a sign... Please, my love, give me a sign—let me know that you are with me... I need a sign...

Mickey knocks something over. Madame suddenly turns and sees him. She think he is her dead husband's ghost. She shrieks and passes out

Mickey exits

The Chief rises to his feet, holding his head. His eye is blackened. He sees Madame and staggers to her aid. Madame is in a happy dream-like state

Chief Madame Celestine, what has happened?
Madame Oh, Chief Inspector... I saw him...
Chief You saw—the villain?
Madame With my own eyes I saw him.
Chief How did he look?
Madame He—he looked at me with those dark, faraway eyes...
Chief You have a description—that is good. (*He takes out his note pad*) Give me the details, Madame.

Scene 2

Madame Handsome ... dark hair ... dark eyes... Tall, but not too tall. Short, but not too short, strong, firm build. But not too strong or too firm ... just right...
Chief Yes. Yes. I have that, Madame. What was he wearing?
Madame (*dreamily*) He was wearing—white.
Chief White!
Madame That is what I said... White.
Chief Strange to wear white. Not a good camouflage.
Madame They all wear white (*she points*) up there.
Chief (*looking up*) He is in the bedroom?
Madame He is higher than the bedroom, Inspector.
Chief The attic! He is in the attic?
Madame No... No... He is...
Chief Where, Madame? Where is the suspect?
Madame (*contentedly*) He is in heaven.
Chief You have killed him, Madame?
Madame No. I could never kill him—I love him.
Chief You love—a rogue and a villain?
Madame George is a rogue yes, but not a villain.
Chief George! That is his name?
Madame Oh course it is his name. It is a name that is always on my lips and in my heart.
Chief I think we had better go through this one more time, Madame. The man you saw had dark hair and dark eyes. He is neither tall or small with firm thighs, he was wearing the colour white and his name is George.

She nods

And he is (*he points*) up there?
Madame Indeed he is. My darling George has been in heaven for many years. I have only his ashes.
Chief Ashes! Madame, are you talking about your husband George?
Madame Of course, who else would I be talking about?
Chief I thought... Oh, never mind... (*He rubs his head*) It has been a very unusual day.

Madame notices his black eye

Madame Oh, my goodness... What has happened to you, Chief Inspector?
Chief You failed to inform me of your new girl, Madame.
Madame (*still dazed*) New girl?
Chief Veronica, the Viking Queen. She is wonderful and a very good boxer. It is very unusual in a woman. I like it...
Madame Boxer! Chief Inspector, perhaps it would be better if you forgot about the diamonds and went home, obviously seeing your wife in bed with another man has affected your mind greatly.
Chief No more so than your allegedly seeing your dead husband, Madame. However, I have thrown myself into my work since finding my wife in bed with her lover. But I am a professional, am I not. I intend to go back to the station to try to uncover more of the suspect's whereabouts. I ask only that you contact me immediately should anything suspicious occur.
Madame Of course, Chief Inspector. Of course.

The Chief exits

Madame speaks to the urn as if she were in a trance

It was so wonderful to see you, my darling, you looked so—so angelic. Your eyes met mine and I was a young woman in love. Please visit me again, my darling, I will close my eyes and concentrate. (*She pauses*) I am waiting for you.

Mickey enters slowly and cautiously, as he is not sure which room he is in. Madame opens her eyes and shrieks with delight

George! My darling George! You have come back.

Mickey stands transfixed, then suddenly decides to make a run for it. He is about to exit when she shouts after him

Scene 2

Please George, don't go! I want to thank you for giving me so many diamonds... Please wait...

On hearing the word "diamonds", Mickey halts abruptly. He pauses to reflect on his next move. He speaks in a "ghostly" Dutch-accented voice

Mickey You have got the diamonds?
Madame (*puzzled*) Of course I have the diamonds! You had them put in the vase, did you not? George, your accent—it is a little strange.
Mickey I do not get much chance to speak Dutch "over here".
Madame Why would you want to speak Dutch—you are an American.
Mickey Over here we speak in many tongues.
Madame Of course. George, I cannot see you under your angelic shroud, but is everything all right—"over there" on the "other side"?
Mickey (*American accent*) Yep. Everything's hunky dory, sweetheart.
Madame I am so glad. Now, my darling, I know that you don't have much time. So is there anything important that you wish to say to me?
Mickey Yup. I want my diamonds back, sweetheart.
Madame Back! But I have only just had them given.
Mickey Yup. Well sugar, that's the way the mop flops. Now be a honey and get the diamonds for me.
Madame Of course, my darling, I will get them for you immediately. (*She moves to get the diamonds*)

Frank enters, still dressed as Veronica

Frank (*to Mickey*) Oh, there you are! I've been looking for you everywhere over there!
Madame Over there! You mean—on the other side? Who are you?

Frank *(pointing at Mickey)* Er—I'm with him.
Madame *(devastated)* You are with my George! *(To Mickey)* You have a woman on the "other side"? How could you do this to me, George? How could you do this, I am overcome with depression... I cannot bear to think of you with another woman. I don't feel well... *(She faints on to the settee)*
Mickey Now look what you've done. She was just about to get the diamonds.
Frank She knows where the diamonds are?
Mickey I reckon the whole bloody lot of 'em know where they are.
Frank What are we going to do?
Mickey I've got to think, got to think! Hang on! I've got it! I've got a plan!
Frank Oh, no! Not another one...!
Mickey Come on! Hurry up! We haven't got much time.

Frank and Mickey exit

Corrine enters cautiously. After making sure that no-one is coming, she tiptoes across to the table, only to discover flowers in the vase. Alarmed, she is about to pick out the flowers when she hears a noise off stage. She hides as best she can

Kora enters cautiously. She tiptoes across to the table and discovers the flowers

She is about to pick out the flowers, when Corrine jumps up and startles her

Corrine Looking for something, chérie?
Kora Oh, you French fool, you startled me!
Corrine What are you doing here?
Kora I am doing nothing! I was merely making sure that the diamonds were still there and that you had not stolen them from me.

Scene 2

Corrine Just as you were going to steal them from me, you greedy Dutch cow. I will look in the vase first.
Kora No. I will look in the vase first.
Corrine (*pulling her back*) No, you will not! I shall look in the vase first. You will get behind me, you Dutch dollop.
Kora One of these days, you Parisian parasite, I shall pull out your fingernails one by one.
Corrine That will be easy, chérie, for you will find them embedded in your neck.

They stop suddenly, as they see the flowers in the vase

Oh no!
Kora What is it? What...?

Madame moans softly from the settee

Corrine It is Madame! She is hurt!

The girls run to her aid. Corrine sits behind Madame to support her

Madame, what is wrong?
Kora Has somebody hit you, Madame?
Madame (*dreamily*) I saw him.
Kora Saw who, Madame?
Madame He looked at me with those dark, dangerous eyes.
Corrine Who? What did he look like?
Madame He was wearing white.
Kora White! It is unusual for a man to wear white!
Madame They all wear white (*she points*) —up there.
Kora Up where, Madame?
Corrine The bedroom, you idiot!
Kora The thief who stole the diamonds is in one of the bedrooms! Oh my God, he's come back for them! What are we going to do?
Corrine (*dropping Madame*) Do? I am getting out of here right now.

Kora So am I! And with the diamonds!
Corrine Oh no, you don't! I will take them with me!

Both girls grab the vase at the same time and begin to tussle with it

Kora Let go!
Corrine You let go! It is mine!
Kora Take your filthy French hands off it!
Corrine You take *your* filthy *Dutch* hands off it!

Frank and Mickey enter. They are dressed in George's suits

Mickey (*to the girls*) What's going on here then?

The girls stop fighting. Madame comes to, but is still rather dazed

Madame Who are you?
Mickey I am Inspector Marks from Scotland Yard.
Madame Inspector Marks of Scotland Yard?
Mickey That's what I said, Madam. And this is my colleague Inspector Spencer.
Madame Inspector Marks and Spencer of Scotland Yard, England?
Mickey Correct. We have been sent to Amsterdam in connection with the theft of a large haul of diamonds.
Kora
Corrine (*together*) Diamonds!

They quickly put down the vase

Frank That's what he said, yeah.
Madame H-how can we help you, Inspectors Marks and Spencer?
Mickey We have reason to believe that the diamonds were hidden somewhere in this establishment.
Madame Hidden in my establishment?
Mickey That's what I said. Hidden. It's imperative that we find

Scene 2

the diamonds before the villains return. I will need to speak to all your staff.
Madame But my girls are busy, Inspector, they cannot leave their windows! Time is money—I cannot afford the time. I...
Mickey (*angrily*) Please, Madam, will you sit down.

She sits down quickly

(*To the girls*) You lot sit down as well.
Kora But I might have a customer.
Corrine So might I and I need the money...
Mickey I said sit down.

The girls sit

Now then. I believe that somebody in this place knows the whereabouts of a certain bag of diamonds. Am I right?

All three look at each other and shrug their shoulders

I see. Nobody wants to talk, hey?
Madame That is because we have nothing to say, Inspector.

The doorbell rings

Mickey Don't answer it.
Madame But I must. It could be a customer. Are you going to pay me what my girls shall lose? Pouf! You will not. (*She opens the door*)

The Chief enters

Chief Good evening, Madame Celestine.
Madame I—I did not expect you back so soon!
Chief I felt I had to return. I could not rid myself of this continual gnawing in the pit of my stomach.

Madame I am sure we can find someone to alleviate that for you.
Chief It is not that kind of pain, Madame. It is caused by the matter I spoke of earlier.
Madame Ah! Everybody wants to discuss *that* matter. Perhaps you should get together with the two Inspectors of Scotland Yard.
Chief Scotland Yard!
Madame They too are interested in *that* matter. This is Inspector Marks and Inspector Spencer. This is Chief Inspector Andre of the Amsterdam Police.
Frank ⎫
Mickey ⎭ (*together*) Chief Inspector!
Madame That is what I said, yes.
Chief Strange that I was not informed of your arrival.
Frank We didn't know you was coming neither. Strange that, init?
Chief (*looking closely at Frank*) Wait a minute... I have the elephant's trunk for remembering faces, I am sure that we have met before.
Frank I—er—I've got that kind of face...
Mickey Well—er, if you'll excuse us, we'll have to be getting on about our business. We've got lots more places to check over...

They head for the front door

I dare say we'll be speaking to you soon, Chief Inspector. Goodbye, Madam.
Chief There is no need to check other premises, my men have already done so.
Frank Yeah, but it's easy to miss a little black pouch of diamonds...

Mickey elbows him in the ribs

What I meant to say was...
Chief How do you know they are in a black pouch?

Scene 2

Frank What?
Mickey Ignore him, Chief Inspector, he's been watching too many films. Come on.
Chief Wait! You will stop right there! I think I would like to check your credentials.
Mickey Oh yeah! Well check this, mate. (*He produces a gun*)

All are horrified

Now get back there and sit down, the lot of you.
Corrine You are not policemen at all! You are the villains who stole the diamonds!
Mickey That's right! Now—which one of you has got my diamonds?

Silence

Don't make me use this.

Silence

OK—I can see I'm going to have to take this one step at a time. (*He approaches Kora menacingly*) Starting with this little tart.
Kora I—I haven't done anything. (*She points to Corrine*) She took the diamonds.
Corrine Liar!
Kora I told her to leave them where they were but she wouldn't listen.
Corrine That is not true, Inspector! She found them and said they were for her alone. I wanted to take them to the station right there and then but she refused.
Kora She is lying! It was I who wanted to give them up!
Mickey Shut up the pair of you! OK, which one of you is going to show me where the diamonds are?
Kora I—she put them in the vase.
Mickey Which vase?
Corrine The vase on the table.

Mickey Have a shufti in the vase, Frank, and don't anyone else move.

Frank checks the vase

Frank Empty.
Kora Empty! (*To Corrine*) You cow! You took the diamonds for yourself!
Corrine Liar! You have taken them for yourself.
Mickey All right, all right, that's enough of that. I'm getting pretty sick of this. (*He points his gun at Corrine*) Were these flowers in the vase when you put the diamonds in?
Corrine ⎫
Kora ⎭ (*together*) No.
Mickey So where did the flowers come from?
Chief I brought them for Madame Celestine.
Corrine Then Madame must have the diamonds.
Madame How dare you implicate me in this!
Mickey OK, lady, where are the diamonds?
Madame I do not know. Believe me I do not know. (*She rushes to the urn, picks it up and holds it to her chest*) Oh George, my darling, tell them to go...
Mickey Will you shut up! Frank, check the vase out.
Madame No! No! It is not a vase, it is an urn! It contains my husband's ashes!
Mickey What better place to hide 'em?
Madame No! It will kill him!
Mickey He's already dead!

Frank snatches the urn from her and tips it upside down over the waste basket. The pouch falls out together with a quantity of black ash

Frank Got 'em.
Mickey Well done, Frank. All right, you lot, into that room.

The girls scream

Scene 2

Shut up, or I'll do the lot of yer.

The others go into the room

OK, Frank, lock the door.

Frank locks the door

Right! We've got what we want, let's go. We'll be miles away before they get out.

Frank and Mickey exit

Noises are heard off stage as the others shout and bang on the door

Chief (*off*) Stand back!

There is a mighty push and the Chief bursts into the room, followed by the others

Madame Well done, Chief Inspector! Well done!
Chief What a fool I was. I know now where I saw the man—it was the woman.
Madame Man—woman, I do not understand.
Chief Veronica. The Viking Queen—it was not a she—it was a he. He and his accomplice—the man you thought was your husband—the man in white—it was they who stole the diamonds.
Madame You mean the angel in white was not my dead husband?
Chief No, Madame—we have both been duped.
Madame And they have gone with the diamonds—scot free. Oh Chief Inspector, this will do your reputation considerable damage. You might even get fired—like these two idiots.
Corrine Fired! But, Madame, it was she...
Kora Do not put the blame on me, you Parisian prat.
Madame Stop it this instant. Get your clothes together and leave my establishment immediately.
Corrine But, Madame...

Madame Go—now.

Kora and Corrine exit glumly

Chief Were you not a little hard on them, Madame Celestine?

Madame I do not think so. They must be taught a lesson for their greed. They should have told me about the diamonds straight away. Had they done so I would have notified you immediately. You would have then caught the villains and been hailed as the greatest Chief Inspector of all time. As it is, you let the villains get away with the diamonds and everyone will know that you bungled the job. You will probably be demoted—perhaps fired.

Chief Fired! But—but I did the best I could in the circumstances, Madame.

Madame Of course you did, Chief Inspector—you could do no more. Of course, it will be difficult to prove that you were not an accomplice also.

Chief An accomplice!

Madame Once the newspapers and television find out that you have let the villains slip through your grasp so easily, they will conjure up all kinds of stories. You know what the media are like. They love a good story even if they know it to be untrue. It would be difficult proving your innocence.

Chief But you would speak for me, Madame?

Madame Of course, but who would believe me, I am a mere brothel keeper, am I not?

Chief I—I am not sure what I should do to alleviate these possible events.

Madame You should go after those villains. You must not let them get away. Follow them to the ends of the earth, if you have to, but you must recover the diamonds at all costs. If not, you can be tarnished for the rest of your life.

Chief The rest of my life?

Madame I would hate to see you publicly humiliated, Chief Inspector. We have been friends for a long time.

Chief You are right, of course. I shall go after them immediately. I must find the villains and recover the diamonds, it is a matter

Scene 2

of my honour. I would not be able to hold my head up in Amsterdam if I were to fail in this mission. Goodbye, Madame. Forgive me for leaving so abruptly...
Madame Do not apologise, Chief Inspector, I understand perfectly. Goodbye and good luck.

He is about to exit when Kora and Corrine enter

Corrine Please, Chief Inspector, would you give me a lift to the station?
Kora And me also?
Corrine I am not sitting with you!
Kora Then get into the boot where you belong, you French whore.
Chief Please, please, ladies, I will be happy to give you both a lift, but I must hurry. I have much to do. Goodbye, Madame Celestine.
Madame Good journey, Chief Inspector. I hope you recover the diamonds—if only for the sake of your honour.
Chief I will not rest until I do.

The Chief, Kora and Corrine exit

Madame waits, looks around to see that nobody is looking, picks up the waste basket and tips it back into the urn

Madame What a terrible thing to do to you, my darling. I hope you were not pained by it. Pouf! And what idiots to think they could outsmart a man such as you. (*She lifts up her skirt and takes the pouch of diamonds from her stocking top*) How wise of you to tell me to switch diamonds. By the time they discover that the diamonds are merely pebbles, we will be out of Amsterdam and on our way to the Riviera. (*She puts the pouch into the urn*) Look after them for me, George, while I pack just a few little things. I will not need much, I will *buy* all I need...

Madame exits

The Lights dim

Scene 3

A few minutes later

A man wearing a balaclava appears at the window. He checks to see that all is clear, then climbs easily in. He is dressed in black and carrying a bag and his movements are that of a professional cat-burglar. Swiftly, he takes the valuables from the room and puts them in his bag. He crosses to the urn, undecided, shrugs his shoulders and throws that in the bag too. When he is satisfied that he has everything worth having, he dashes back to the window and clambers out. Dustbins rattle and footsteps are heard running away

Madame enters, carrying a suitcase and wearing a hat and coat. She crosses to the mantelpiece to collect the urn, not realizing that it has been stolen

Madame I am ready, my darling. Oh, I cannot wait to get away from here for a while. A holiday will do me. (*She notices that the urn is missing*) What...! Where have you gone, my darling...? (*She looks around the room and notices that everything has gone. She rushes to the window, notices a man running in the street*) Come back! Come back, you bastard! How dare you steal my diamonds! Stop that man! (*She realizes that it is too late and slumps miserably against the window*)

Police sirens and running footsteps are heard as the chase begins outside

CURTAIN

FURNITURE AND PROPERTY LIST

Further dressing may be added at the director's discretion

Scene 1

On stage: Settee
Table. *On it:* vase
Chair
Bar. *On it:* water jug, glasses, drinks including brandy
Mantelpiece. *On it:* urn containing black ash, pot with artificial plant
Waste basket

Off stage: Bunch of flowers (**Chief**)

Personal: **Frank:** map, pouch of diamonds
Madame: book

Scene 2

On stage: As before

Off stage: Whip (**Frank**)

Personal: **Chief:** note pad, pen
Mickey: gun
Madame: pouch of diamonds

SCENE 3

On stage: As before

Off stage: Suitcase (**Madame**)
Bag (**Cat-burglar**)

Personal: **Madame:** hat

LIGHTING PLOT

Property fittings required: nil
1 interior. The same throughout

SCENE 1	Night

To open: Overall general lighting

Cue 1   Footsteps heard off stage   (Page 2)
Flashing lights outside the window

Cue 2   **Madame**: "...of them for me, my darling."   (Page 11)
Black-out

SCENE 2   Evening

To open: Dim lighting

Cue 3   **Madame** exits   (Page 31)
Dim lights

SCENE 3   Evening

To open: Dim lighting

*No cue*s

EFFECTS PLOT

Cue 1	To open *Sounds of police chase: sirens blaring; car doors slamming; footsteps running, getting closer and closer, finally coming to a halt*	(Page 1)
Cue 2	**Mickey**: "Let's get in, quick!" *Dustbins rattle*	(Page 1)
Cue 3	**Mickey**: "…on your shoulders." *Dustbins rattle*	(Page 2)
Cue 4	**Frank** and **Mickey** hide in front of settee *Footsteps running off stage*	(Page 2)
Cue 5	Lights flash outside the window *Fade footsteps down*	(Page 2)
Cue 6	**Mickey**: "Ssh!" *Fade out footsteps*	(Page 2)
Cue 7	**Frank** and **Mickey** exit, crashing dustbins *Cat's hiss and meow*	(Page 4)
Cue 8	**Kora**: "Do your snorting elsewhere!" *Footsteps, fading into distance*	(Page 4)
Cue 9	**Madame**: "…enable me to get more money?" *Doorbell rings*	(Page 9)

Effects Plot

Cue 10	To open Scene 2 *Footsteps. Dustbins clang*	(Page 12)
Cue 11	**Madame** is about to pour herself a drink *Doorbell rings*	(Page 12)
Cue 12	**Madame**: "…nothing to say, Inspector." *Doorbell rings*	(Page 25)
Cue 13	**Cat-burglar** clambers out *Dustbins rattle. Footsteps of man running away*	(Page 32)
Cue 14	**Madame** slumps against window *Police sirens and running footsteps*	(Page 32)

www.ingramcontent.com/pod-product-compliance
Lightning Source LLC
Chambersburg PA
CBHW070453050426
42450CB00012B/3256

Running from Amsterdam police, diamond thieves Frank and Mickey find an open window, clamber inside, and discover they are in a brothel! They hide the diamonds and escape, planning to return later. Two working girls, Corrine and Kora, find the diamonds and move them to a vase, but their boss, Madame Celestine, finds them in turn and vows to keep them. Chaos ensues!

| CASTING | 3 women, 4 men, 2 women or men |

SAMUEL FRENCH *Acting* Editions

samuelfrench.co.uk
samuelfrenchltd
samuel french uk

ISBN 9780573122187

HOUSEKEEPER WANTED

By
PHILIP KING
FALKLAND L. CARY

SAMUEL FRENCH